Doing the Right Thing

Doing the Right Thing

Sometimes Difficult, but Always Correct

Dewitt Jones, EdD

ROWMAN & LITTLEFIELD
Lanham • Boulder • New York • London

Published by Rowman & Littlefield
An imprint of The Rowman & Littlefield Publishing Group, Inc.
4501 Forbes Boulevard, Suite 200, Lanham, Maryland 20706
www.rowman.com

86-90 Paul Street, London EC2A 4NE

British Library Cataloguing in Publication Information Available

Library of Congress Cataloging-in-Publication Data

Names: Jones, Dewitt, 1947- author.
Title: Doing the right thing : sometimes difficult, but always correct /
  Dewitt Jones.
Description: Lanham, Maryland : Rowman & Littlefield Publishers, [2023]
Identifiers: LCCN 2023004891 (print) | LCCN 2023004892 (ebook) | ISBN
  9781475871296 (cloth) | ISBN 9781475871302 (paperback) | ISBN
  9781475871319 (ebook)
Subjects: LCSH: School principals--United States. | School principals--
  United States--Anecdotes. | School superintendents--United States. | School
  management and organization--United States. | Educational leadership--
  United States.
Classification: LCC LB2831.92 .J67 2023 (print) | LCC LB2831.92 (ebook) |
  DDC 371.2/0120973–dc23/eng/20230302
LC record available at https://lccn.loc.gov/2023004891
LC ebook record available at https://lccn.loc.gov/2023004892

♾™ The paper used in this publication meets the minimum requirements of
American National Standard for Information Sciences—Permanence of Paper for
Printed Library Materials, ANSI/NISO Z39.48-1992.

I want to thank every teacher, student, administrator, college professor, parent, community, and family for being part of my educational journey. It has been a terrific experience and one that changed my life for the better daily.

Contents

Preface

In my over fifty years as a school administrator and teaching in higher education, I felt teaching theory into practice wasn't always happening at higher education levels. So giving professors a supplemental resource—and helping future leaders understand how essential it is to always try to do the right thing in challenging situations—is at the heart of this book.

The scenarios presented in the book, followed by solutions used by administrators, will help future leaders and even current leaders understand the difficulties they will face when making decisions. These decisions could affect not only the people in the scenario but potentially an entire school or district.

The book allows the reader to discuss many of these scenarios and agree or disagree with the presented solutions. As I wrote the book, the scenarios reminded me of how quickly problems that were not dealt with became severe and the lack of administrators doing the right thing caused issues to mushroom out of control.

Finally, I have seen administrators look the other way and not want to deal with serious situations. These administrators have short careers as their lack of decision-making catches up with them quickly. *Doing the Right Thing: Sometimes Difficult, but Always Correct* will help future and current administrators understand how critical their decisions are in serious situations.

Introduction

This book contains real-life scenarios from different districts in different states. The names of everyone involved in the scenarios are fictitious, and the school districts are not named. However, in our lives as school administrators, there will be plenty of situations that cause us to question what to do.

- Most scenarios are simple, but some will be a challenge.
- Some scenarios have political implications.
- Some solutions will potentially upset half the people and please others.
- Some scenarios will have legal impacts. Some will require school board approval.
- Some scenarios are gut wrenching.
- Some scenarios are painful.
- Some scenarios will break your heart.

The common denominator is that when we recognize the right thing to do, we must do that and never bend. It is always correct!

The book's format is straightforward.

- Scenarios in part 1 will be presented without what actions were done by the administrator.
- The reader will think about what they would do and answer the study questions.
- If the reader is in a class studying to be a school administrator, they can weigh in together on potential responses or solutions.

- What the administrator did in each scenario will be presented in part 2, labeled with the same scenario title.
- The reader or class can compare their solutions and agree or disagree with the solutions presented by the administrator.
- Obviously, what is right for one person may not be right for everyone.

Special note: Each scenario solution will identify applicable Professional Standards for Educational Leaders (PSEL). See National Policy Board for Educational Administration (NPBEA), *Professional Standards for Educational Leaders* (Reston, VA: NPBEA, 2015).

PART I

Scenarios

Scenario 1

Loaded Gun in Elementary School

The superintendent, Dr. Samantha Curry, was sitting in her office, returning from visiting a middle school earlier. Then, at 8:30 a.m., her administrative assistant poked her head in and said, "I have an emergency call from the elementary principal at our year-round school. She sounds alarmed."

"Dr. Curry. I need you to come over right away. We had a third-grade boy bring a loaded gun to school. The school resource officer [SRO] is here, but I need you quickly." Dr. Curry hung up, jumped in her SUV, and took off. What was a normal fifteen-minute drive took her ten minutes. As superintendent, she had a lot to consider; her mind was all over the place, thinking about everything, not knowing more than what the principal had shared.

She entered the office, went to Ms. Maya Andrews's office, and sat down. The SRO and the school guidance counselor were also present. Maya started, "As the bus was unloading children this morning, a boy raced to the office and said he was sitting next to his friend Joey and Joey opened his backpack and showed him a pistol that he said was loaded. He further shared that even though he was a friend, he remembered to share it with the office quickly if he saw something bad. So I asked him to sit with the secretary as I didn't want to start a panic."

Ms. Andrews continued, "I called the SRO to come over and then you, Dr. Curry. The SRO went to the locker and brought the backpack to the office, and there was a loaded .22-caliber pistol. I went to the classroom and asked Joey to come with me to the counselor's office. That's where we are now, but there are complications."

The counselor began, "Two weeks ago, there was a fire at Joey's rented home late at night. It was all over the television and in the newspapers. His mother's boyfriend was at work. Mom got Joey out of the house but could not get his two siblings out before the fire department arrived, and they died. As a result, Joey has been in counseling with the Department of Social Services and me three times a week."

Maya then said, "As we all know, the state law says that bringing a loaded gun to school is automatic expulsion. The rest of the story will explain why there is no way I can recommend expulsion, and I know it is out of my hands. That's why you are here, Dr. Curry."

The counselor shared, "Joey had an appointment with me at 9:00 a.m. today. He explained with the SRO present that they moved to another home after the fire. The boyfriend was hitting his mother, and Joey knew he had a gun in the kitchen drawer. So after the fight, Joey took the gun, placed it in a ziplock baggie, and buried it in the backyard so the boyfriend couldn't shoot his mom. He then worried that the boyfriend would hurt his mother if he couldn't find the gun the next day, thinking she had taken it. So he put it in his backpack and was going to give it to his counselor at his 9:00 a.m. appointment."

Everyone all sat back. Maya expressed that if Joey were expelled, it would ruin his life forever. The SRO shared that there must be a way around expulsion, but he was in no position to do anything. Maya looked at Dr. Curry and said, "Whatever will happen must happen quickly, as this is a big deal. You are the only person who can now deal with this situation, Dr. Curry."

She added, "Here is a copy of the letter home to parents explaining that a student brought a gun to school, and it was quickly recovered, and the student will not return to our school. If you find a way to avoid expulsion, I will contact the previous elementary school he attended in our district and talk to the principal. Keep me posted."

***

You are the superintendent of this large urban school district. In this case, the elementary school was the district's highest free- and reduced-lunch building. It was a year-round school with a minority population of over 90 percent. Joey was an intelligent African American student with tremendous potential.

- What will you do?
- What are the issues?
- What decisions will you make?
- Who will you contact?
- How fast will you act?
- What about the state laws/requirements?

See what happened in part 2, "Scenario Solutions." Don't peek before you answer or finish discussing all the questions! Doing the right thing is hard, and this is one of the hardest!

Scenario 2

Drum Line

Moving to a suburban high school as a new principal, replacing the retired principal of fifteen years, was an interesting experience for Mr. Jason McMillan. The arts had been ignored for some time, and the district had hired a new band director, one of Iowa's best. His goal was to change the program's image quickly.

Homecoming was exciting as the football team was ranked number one in the state by then. The events' planning was extensive, including a community and school pep assembly, community and student parade, king and queen voting, the football game, and the dance.

The district let out at 12:20 p.m., and the community/school pep assembly began at 1:30 p.m. in the school gym. The planning for the assembly had started a month before the event. The cheerleading sponsor was in charge of organizing the assembly and had done so for eight years.

The new band director attended one of the planning committee meetings, asking what role the band would have in the assembly. He was told by the cheerleading sponsor, "The band will sit in the corner across from the main bleachers and play the school song at the program's start and the end. Nothing else."

The new director explained that he had formed a drum line and wanted them to perform at some point in the program besides the school song. However, the cheerleading sponsor said, "The band is terrible, and I will not allow them to do more than they ever have at this event."

The director was more than upset when he came into Mr. McMillan's office. First, he explained what the sponsor had told him. Then he asked, "Mr. McMillan, this drumline is awesome and will bring the house down. What can you do to help?"

***

Okay—you are the new principal. What are you going to do?

- Who will you talk to?
- Do you contact the central office?
- Is this a political issue?
- Is the cheerleading sponsor right?
- Who will you involve?

By the way, this was a much larger issue than ever imagined!

Scenario 3

Motorcycle Ride

Middle school students go through many changes during that time in their lives. One of the common phrases used to describe kids at this tender age is "feet and hormones." They are growing fast and sometimes falling over themselves, and as their hormones kick in, they are experiencing new emotions and feelings for the first time. In this scenario, the district's third-year middle school principal, James Carter, had to start an investigation involving a student making a charge of inappropriate touching by a teacher.

Ned Aldrich had just graduated from college and was excited to start his teaching career as the new seventh-grade social studies teacher. Making the leap from a student in May to a teacher in September was easy for him. The faculty and student body immediately accepted him as a warm and friendly teacher. Ned was a sharp dresser and a handsome young man as well. The students also thought it was cool that he rode a motorcycle when the weather permitted. He also coached seventh-grade football and planned to coach basketball when that season arrived.

Ned's classroom management and teaching skills were good for a first-year teacher. Students knew his expectations, and he worked hard to ensure that all his students succeeded. After school, he would stay to help kids who needed assistance, and he even started a morning study session for those interested.

Many weekends for Ned were spent going back to his university to visit his girlfriend, who was a senior. In October, about five weeks into the school year, Ned's girlfriend came with him to a Friday night home football game. The middle school kids didn't know her, and since he hadn't mentioned her, they were all very curious. So instead of having a lot of time to watch the game, Ned and his girlfriend spent most of the first quarter by the concession stand visiting with his students.

The following Monday morning, at about 9:00 a.m., Melissa, a seventh-grade student, went to the counselor's office in tears and asked to speak to her. After her conversation with Melissa, Ms. Becker came to the principal's office with the following account by Melissa:

Melissa, who lived about two blocks from Mr. Aldrich's apartment, walked by just as he left on Saturday afternoon on his motorcycle. He asked her if she had ever ridden on a motorcycle. She said no, and he invited her to take a short ride to the middle school, where he would pick up some work to bring home. When they got to the middle school, Melissa asked Mr. Aldrich when the new addition under construction would be completed. He told her about six months but that if she wanted to see the nearly enclosed part, he would walk her into that part before going to his classroom.

When they got inside the enclosed construction area, Melissa said that Mr. Aldrich hugged her, took down his pants, and asked her to touch him, which she said she did. They then went to his classroom to get his work, and he took her home.

Ms. Becker took notes as Melissa told the story and explained that she would have to go to the principal's office and share the information. Melissa said she understood, and the guidance office secretary was asked to sit in the room with Melissa while Ms. Becker came to the office.

When Ms. Becker finished reading the account that Melissa had given her, Mr. Carter asked her what she thought. Ms. Becker said that Melissa told her the story three times, and each version was the same, with only a few minor added or deleted comments. In her twenty years as a school counselor, she had heard kids give similar accounts and felt that Melissa's story seemed credible.

Ms. Becker went back to the guidance office to be with Melissa. Mr. Carter called Ned into his office and sent a paraprofessional into Ned's classroom to watch the kids. He was asked if he had given Melissa a ride on his motorcycle Saturday afternoon, and he said yes. Next, he was asked if he had taken her to the middle school and shown her the new construction site, and he said yes. Then, finally, had he taken her to his classroom to get work and then taken her home? He said yes. The principal then shared with him what Melissa claimed to have happened at the construction site, and Ned was utterly shocked, instantly denying her story.

Ned was then told that he needed to write down exactly what had happened Saturday and that he used very poor judgment by giving her a ride on his motorcycle, taking her to the construction site, and being alone with her. He understood and said that Melissa seemed lonely at school, didn't have a lot of friends, and had confided in him about her parents going through a divorce that summer; he felt sorry for her. However, he never even thought about the possibility of her fabricating such a story or accusing him of something so terrible.

As a young administrator, Mr. Carter needed assistance with this issue and asked the high school principal to meet with him to discuss the next steps. Clearly, there was the possibility that Mr. Aldrich had done precisely what Melissa had accused him of doing. But unfortunately, this was 1975, and the current processes we use today for this situation did not exist. So the high school principal and Mr. Carter wrote a strategy to follow, and then the investigation began.

***

You are the principal. Knowing that there are serious issues for the future of the teacher as well as the student, what are your next steps?

- What should be included in the strategy that you and the high school principal develop? What are the issues?
- Should the school attorney be contacted?
- Should the police be contacted?
- Should you advise Mr. Aldrich to contact an attorney?
- Who will contact the parents and when?
- How fast should this situation be resolved? Is this even a problem?

This was a tough problem for a young principal. Before you read the solution, put yourself in his position as you review the questions above.

Scenario 4

Arena Conferences

Missing Teacher

In his first year as the new high school principal in a suburban school district, the learning curve was very steep for Dr. Robert Ford. After the first nine weeks came to a close, parent-teacher conferences were scheduled. This high school used an arena conference format, meaning that the lunchroom was where tables were set up for each teacher with their names prominently displayed in alphabetical order. Adjacent rooms were also available for parents or teachers who wanted privacy.

Everything was fine until Dr. Ford noticed an empty table with parents lined up, expecting to see Ms. Wheeler, but she was not there. So he went to her social studies department chair and asked if she had been notified that Ms. Wheeler would be late or not attending. The department chair explained that she had heard nothing but that this wasn't the first time she had just not shown up for conferences, and the previous principal had not taken any action to the best of her knowledge.

The principal immediately went to the office and called Ms. Wheeler, but there was no answer. Then, he went back to her table with a form that each parent wanting to meet with Ms. Wheeler could sign with their phone number so the teacher could schedule a time to visit. But unfortunately, this was in the fall of 1987, so cell phones were unavailable.

Dr. Ford asked Ms. Wheeler to see him during her planning period the following day. His assistant principal was also present at the conference. Ms. Wheeler explained that she was on her way to conferences and had an accident on the corner of Fifth and University. She further explained that she was shaken up and had just returned to her home and

13

tried to contact the office, but no one answered. Finally, she said, "I intended to see you over my lunch hour to tell you what had happened."

The principal handed her the sheet of parents wanting to speak to her and asked her to please get in touch with them within seven school days, mark the sheet with the dates and times of her calls, and turn it into the office. She left in a huff. The assistant principal said she didn't believe a word, but it would be her word against theirs if they administered any discipline.

***

You are the high school principal of this large suburban high school.

- What are the issues?
- What decisions will you make?
- Will you involve Ms. Wheeler's department chair?
- Who will you contact?
- How fast will you act?
- Could discipline be appropriate for this teacher?

Find out what happened in the solutions section of the book. Don't peek before you answer or discuss all the questions!

Scenario 5

Newspaper Conflict

The old adage "Never get into an argument with someone who buys ink by the barrel" refers to newspapers. Unfortunately, it is accurate, and no one wins when you get upset with your local newspapers.

As superintendent in a large urban district, Dr. Cassie Martin had established an excellent relationship with the editorial board of the daily newspaper. As a result, the district's team met with their team monthly, shared information, and answered questions.

In her second year in the district, as she scanned the daily newspaper, she read a tiny article deep in the newspaper about the neighboring district's high school. Two students had been arrested at school for possession of drugs with intent to deliver. This was a serious situation, and the students would be brought up for expulsion, besides the legal troubles they would face.

The student population of this district was utterly different from the superintendent's district. Her district's free- and reduced-lunch rate was about 87 percent, and the minority population was 42 percent. The student population spoke over twenty other languages in the district. It was great to have all the diversity. The neighboring community was affluent, and a state university was at the heart of their district.

Three months later, two high school students in the highest minority high school population in Dr. Martin's district were arrested at school for possession of drugs with intent to deliver. The well-read local newspaper reported the story on the front page, above the fold. The headline was in one-inch bold letters.

***

You are the superintendent. Based on the information presented:

- What are your next steps?
- Who will you involve?
- Can you maintain a good relationship with the newspaper? Is this important?
- You are close friends with the neighboring superintendent. Will you involve him in your decision?
- Will you communicate with your school board regarding this situation?

This is a complicated scenario. Dr. Martin did the right thing for herself and the district, but she was cautious. Have fun with this one. It is a great group discussion topic. See the solution at the back of the book! Reminder—don't peek!

Scenario 6

Parent Demand

In his first week as principal in a reasonably large suburban high school, Dr. William Cassidy met with the only other person working in July. Geoff was the guidance counselor in charge of scheduling and was very proud that the computer program had taken care of 91 percent of all student requests. After that, it entailed doing it by hand, contacting students with unresolvable conflicts, and asking them what choices they wanted to consider.

Geoff was really good at this, and one rule he preached was that any student who wanted to move from second-period math to fourth-period math would have their request honored if they requested to switch to a smaller class section. But, of course, moving to a larger class section was never approved.

The next day, Geoff came into the office and said a parent wanted his son to be switched from the seventh-hour physical education class on Tuesday and Thursday to the second period, where he currently had a study hall. Second-period PE was a larger class section than seventh period. In addition, his son worked daily at a mall and needed the change made. Geoff explained that if the change were granted for his son, there would be seventy-eight other denied requests that would have to be given equal treatment.

Dr. Cassidy was the person in charge of scheduling at his previous high school. Geoff's concerns were accurate, and the principal told him, "You have my complete support for your decision." Sure enough, the father of the student came in the next day.

None of the secretarial staff started until August 1, so Dr. Cassidy was sitting at one of their front desks doing work. Then, a man entered the office. "My name is Joseph Guzzy, and I'm sure the counselor has already explained my request for our son to move his PE class to second period so he can go to work at the mall earlier after school."

Dr. Cassidy stood up. "Let's go to my office, Mr. Guzzy, so we can have some privacy if someone else comes in."

Mr. Guzzy continued, "I know the rules regarding switching sections, but who cares about PE class numbers? I have volunteered tons of time helping in your schools and purchased over twenty computers for the business department. In addition, I am a prominent attorney, was named Citizen of the Year, and rode on the first float in the July Fourth parade. So I expect my request to be honored."

Dr. Cassidy grew up in a wealthy northern Chicago suburb, similar to this community. In an immensely rich and political area folks wanted things their way no matter what.

"Mr. Guzzy, did the counselor explain what would happen if he honored your request?"

"Yes, he did, and if you approve this, our family will tell no one."

"That's not the point, Mr. Guzzy. Almost one hundred students would have to be given the same options your son had."

"I need my request to be honored, Dr. Cassidy."

***

You are the principal. Doing the right thing may alienate this prominent parent, but making the change will become public for sure. What will you do?

- This is your first month on the job; who else can you contact?
- Can you justify the change as it is only PE?
- What are your options?

Scenario 7

Marching Band Sousaphones

Starting any job as a school administrator has its complications. In Dr. Mason Hicks's first week as the superintendent in a large urban school district—two traditional high schools, an alternative high school, four middle schools, and thirteen elementary schools—there were more differences between the two traditional high schools than expected.

One high school was on the east side of town and predominately in a medium- to low-income area. On the city's west side, the high school was a medium- to upper-income area. The alternative high school drew students from both high schools. At the end of his first week, the east side high school band director, Joel Mueller, came to see Dr. Hicks.

He introduced himself, and they had a lot in common, as Dr. Hicks's first job teaching was as a former band director. Joel explained, "I know I am overstepping the chain of command, but I have a unique problem. Our band program is growing, and marching band season is starting soon. I have only one marching sousaphone, and three additional students who are registered from two middle schools play the sousaphone. I went to the music boosters, and they have no money, and a fundraiser will not cover the $12,000 cost for the instruments."

Dr. Hicks asked, "Did you talk to your principal?"

Joel smiled and answered, "That's why I'm here. She said she could not afford $12,000 and should come to the district office and talk to someone. I don't want to tell these three freshmen that they can't be in the band because we don't have the sousaphones and can't afford them. This is a message they always hear at school and in their homes."

"There has to be a way for us to come up with the funds," the superintendent answered.

19

"If we tried a fundraiser, we would only raise probably $2,000. The other high school could sell pizzas on the weekend and raise $20,000."

Clearly, there was a problem that needed to be rectified. "Let me walk down to the business manager's office and explain the situation." The business manager told the superintendent he would transfer $12,000 to the high school's instrumental music department.

When Dr. Hicks returned to his office, he told Joel, "You have $12,000 in your account, so go ahead and purchase the sousaphones."

Joel was delighted, shook his hand, and left the office. Of course, not everything goes this easy, but everything must be done to try to help all students. Dr. Hicks's administrative assistant also expressed her thanks; she could evidently hear the conversation as the office door was open.

Two days later, the administrative assistant said, "Dr. Hicks, you have a phone call from the president of the music boosters on the west side. Do you want the call, or should I take a message?" He told her to put it through.

Janice Willows welcomed the superintendent to the district and explained, "I understand you put $12,000 into the east side high school's band account, and we expect the same thing to be done for our band program."

Their marching band program was one of the best in the Midwest, winning state and midwestern marching band contests. She continued, "Our monthly instrumental booster club meeting is next Tuesday at 6:00 p.m. Would you please attend and explain what you plan to do to make things equal?"

"Thanks for your call, Ms. Willows. I will attend your meeting."

***

Now it is your turn. You are the new superintendent.

- Who will you talk to before the meeting?
- Is Ms. Willows's request reasonable?
- Will you bring anyone with you to the meeting? If so, who?
- Will you tell your board president about the situation?
- Could this be a very political issue?
- Will the press be at the meeting?
- What will be your decision regarding the music boosters' request?

Scenario 8

Closing an Elementary School

In an urban school district, one of the superintendent's responsibilities is always looking to the future when making critical decisions. Dr. Cynthia Mason's announcement of her intention to retire the next fiscal school year gave the school board plenty of time to hire a search firm and appoint her successor. However, the superintendent knew that the district had too many elementary schools and needed to close one so the new superintendent would not face a controversial first-year decision.

After careful study by the district facilities committee composed of two school board members, two architects, the district facilities director, the city engineer, and three administrators, the team agreed they needed to close one elementary school. In addition, the team had commissioned a demographic study by a firm in Kansas City, and the results confirmed that they could close one elementary school and send those children to three different buildings, all of which had plenty of room.

Using all the metrics about all the elementary schools, it was apparent that one of the buildings in the poorest physical condition was first on the list. The district had remodeled three buildings and built five new elementary schools as part of the ten-year facilities plan. The issue that would make it very controversial was that the chosen elementary school had the highest free- and reduced-lunch rate and the highest minority population.

The school board knew that the politics of this closure recommendation would cause public resistance and divide the community. Therefore, a public meeting was scheduled at a middle school close to the elementary school in question. All the data were presented, including by experts regarding the physical condition of the targeted building. Superintendent Mason led the meeting, and at the end of all the presentations, it was time for questions from the audience, which numbered probably around six hundred.

Since this was only a recommendation, the community was adamant that the proposal was terrible and was made because of the student population, not because of the condition of the building. They honestly did not trust the school board and wanted the "real" reasons to be stated. Unfortunately, nothing anyone could say at this hearing would change anything. The school board president lived in this attendance area and was being pressured with letters to the editor and personal phone calls.

The proposal was on the following two school board agendas for discussion only.

***

You are the superintendent. What will you do?

- What are the issues?
- Will you change the recommendation and select an alternative elementary school for closure?
- Will the support of the board continue on the proposal?
- What role will the press play? Will they take a position on the proposal?

You will appreciate how complicated this became when you read the solution!

Scenario 9

Receptionist and Maintenance Assistant

This scenario was one of the most demanding challenges. As you read this, please put yourself in the role of superintendent. Then, when you read the solution later, you will understand why.

Mondays always seem to bring interesting issues to any administrator's desk. Superintendent Dr. Toby Johnston started his day at a middle school by visiting the principal, touring the building, and stopping into classrooms. Starting the day, seeing teachers and kids was one of his favorite things to do.

When he returned to his office at 9:00 a.m., the director of operational services was waiting in the outer office. Of course, that was never a good thing; if the superintendent needed to visit with the director, he would go to the director's office. He knew something was amiss.

"Good morning, Dr. Johnston. You might want to sit down when I tell you something that happened this weekend in our administrative center."

"It can't be that bad, Jason."

"Yes, it can!"

Jason sat down in the superintendent's office, and he began sharing. "Before everyone comes into the central office on Monday, one of my guys sweeps the building, just checking if everything is all right. Many of our central office workers stop in and do work over the weekend while it is quiet, just like you. As my guy checked the bathrooms, he found a pair of women's underwear in the upstairs women's lounge. There is a long vinyl bench/couch in that lounge, where the underwear was found. He put them in a plastic bag, and I have them in my office."

"Could someone just have changed clothes and left them?" Dr. Johnston was hoping that would be the case.

"As you know, there are cameras at every entrance, as well as in the lobby. They are motion activated and recorded until the motion stops. At 10:00 a.m. yesterday, a receptionist, Sherry, entered the building from the south doors and went upstairs. One hour later, one of my lead assistants came in the lobby door, and the camera didn't show him taking either of the stairs to the second floor, but the camera wasn't focused on the elevator he had to use. There have been rumors that he and the receptionist have been having an affair, but no solid proof. Furthermore, he is categorized as one of her supervisors, which could worsen matters."

Jason continued, "Forty-five minutes after my guy arrived, the receptionist exited the building the same way she had entered. Thirty minutes after she left, my guy exited the building the same way he came in."

The superintendent sat back in his chair and watched as Jason showed him the videos. "You were right, Jason. This could be quite an issue. What a way to start a Monday!"

Jason explained that his guy, Kenny, had been in the district for twenty-five years and was loved by everyone and well respected in the community. He was married with adult kids, and the receptionist was single.

"Dr. Johnston, I will do whatever you want me to. But we would only have a 'he said, she said' situation."

"Let's bring in the assistant superintendent in charge of Human Resources, share all of this with her, and go from there. I'll let you know when we can meet."

After Jason left, Dr. Johnston called his assistant superintendent in Human Resources, Dr. Williams, and asked her if she had any time before lunch. He wanted to talk with her before they brought Jason back. She indicated that she was able to visit at 10:30 a.m.

When Dr. Williams came in at 10:30 a.m., he brought her up to speed on what Jason had shared. Sherry was part of her department, as was Kenny. So she had a vested interest in discussing this situation.

Dr. Williams said, "We need more to move forward on any disciplinary action. Questioning them now will only cause them to say nothing, and then they will get their stories straight, and we will never get to the bottom of anything. So tell Jason that we need to wait and keep our eyes and ears open before getting together."

Dr. Johnston thanked her and got back to the business at hand. On Thursday, the receptionist, Sherry, asked Dr. Johnston's administrative assistant if she could talk to the superintendent. The administrative assistant always requested the nature of the request, and the receptionist said she was uncomfortable sharing. However, since the superintendent was busy when Sherry made the request, his assistant said he was available at 1:00 p.m.

Dr. Williams was asked to attend the meeting, which started promptly at 1:00 p.m. Sherry came in and was in tears as she shared, "I am embarrassed to say that I have been having a consensual affair with Kenny. He promised he was getting a divorce, but I found out that was a lie. Last Sunday, we met in the upstairs women's lounge, and after sex, he told me our relationship was over. I want to file a formal complaint on Kenny as he is one of my supervisors."

***

You are a superintendent. What are your next steps?

- What are the issues?
- Are there any legal ramifications?
- Is this a "he said, she said" situation?
- Do you contact your school attorney?
- What happens if Kenny denies everything?
- What can you prove?

This is a highly complex scenario, and the solution was, as Dr. Williams said, "Crazy!" But it was the right thing!

Scenario 10

Flag Girls

Having a background in the arts was one of the reasons Sam Cook was hired as high school principal at a high school famous for its athletic programs and wanting more emphasis on the arts. The spring before starting his new job, the district hired probably one of the state's best band directors. He was able to take the position before the second semester was over.

That gave him a chance to organize everything that goes into a terrific marching band. The program had never had flag girls, and the director held tryouts. Afterward, all the band members, flag girls, and parents were given a schedule of dates for the fall marching band season. The dates included all the home football games and three marching band contests.

The flag team members were expected to perform on all the listed dates unless they were sick or had a family emergency. Two alternates practiced with the team in case of an absence. All the team members and their parents signed and agreed on the expectations.

Two flag girls approached the band director on the Monday before the third home football game. They told him they had been invited to homecoming at a neighboring school district and would miss the Friday game and the Saturday evening contest. The director reminded the girls that they had committed to the dates and that their reason was unacceptable, and they would be dropped from the squad as per their signed agreement.

The band director came to Mr. Cook and explained the situation. The principal told him, "You have my full support." The parents went to the band director, upset with his decision to drop the girls from the team and put the alternates in their place. They would take this to the principal.

When they came to Mr. Cook's office, they were still upset, and he made matters worse when he told them he supported the director's decision. They told him he hadn't heard the last of this, and their daughters would not be dropped from the squad. "Who do you think you are?" They stomped out of his office.

Most high schools don't usually have evening activities on Wednesdays, as locals churches have evening religious programs for kids. Shortly after Principal Cook got home at 5:00 p.m. and sat down with his wife, someone knocked on the front door. When he answered the door, his superintendent held a six-pack of beer, saying, "We need to talk."

They walked to the deck behind his house and sat down. "So what's so important you had to buy beer and come over?"

"Well, I know you have had the parents of the flag team girls who were dropped from the squad come to see you, and according to them, you support the band director's position. Do I have it right?"

"Yes, you have it right."

"I'm here to require you to tell the band director he has to reverse the decision to drop the two flag girls from the squad."

"Can I ask what your rationale is for this decision?"

"Come on. It's just flag girls, for gosh sake."

***

What will you do as the high school principal? The superintendent isn't giving you an option. You are new to the district.

- What will you tell the band director?
- What will you do next?

Scenario 11

Bus Driver

This scenario will be something you will never forget. Superintendent Dr. Jonathan Murry started his position in 1990. Harold was one of the bus drivers on daily morning and afternoon routes and the varsity baseball team driver for all the away games and tournaments. The kids and coaches loved him, and he was very responsible. He was always on time and volunteered for field trips during the school days.

Things changed for Harold one spring when his son was pulling his younger brother on a skateboard behind his bicycle. The younger brother fell off the skateboard and hit his head on the curb. He was not wearing a helmet. It was a fluke accident that Harold's son did not survive. When that happened, Harold changed.

He still was driving buses just like before the accident, but his personal life was falling apart. He had buttons made of his deceased son and made his other children and wife wear them daily. If they forgot, he would become upset. The school's transportation director had to talk with him a few times about rumors affecting his ability to drive. Things settled down.

The transportation director discovered that Harold and his wife had separated, and he had to leave his home. Court records showed that Harold was arrested on May 25, 1991, for domestic abuse and was placed on probation. On September 5, 1992, he was charged with violating an order to stay away from his home. Not long after that, he was charged with harassing his wife. A divorce was pending.

Harold had continued to drive buses and was looking forward to summer baseball. Then, one morning in the early spring, the transportation director came to the superintendent's office and shared, "Dr.

Murry, there is a rumor that Harold is living in his station wagon and has a gun."

"Is he driving a bus right now?"

"Yes. He is driving a field trip that leaves in thirty minutes from an elementary school."

"Get another driver and take them to the elementary school, and I will meet you both there."

***

So you are the superintendent. Respond to the questions. What is the right thing to do?

- Do you contact the police to go with you to the bus waiting for a field trip?
- What do you tell Harold regarding the rumor of a gun?
- Do you continue to let Harold drive daily routes?
- Do you let Harold keep his baseball driving assignment?
- Do you notify your board members about the situation?

Scenario 12

Superintendent's Daughter

As a third-year high school principal, Henry Carver, now comfortable in the position, knew all the pitfalls and had a terrific relationship with faculty, parents, and the community. The district administrative team was strong, and all the principals trusted each other but did have some issues with the central office. Sometimes the team expected to be supported, and to their surprise, that didn't always happen.

On a Monday morning in March, one of the three counselors, Kyle, entered Mr. Carver office, shut the door, and sat down. He was distraught, saying, "Linda, our superintendent's daughter, is in my office saying that her father was upset with her and took a shorthand broom with a wooden handle and hit her multiple times as she scrambled up to her bedroom last night. Her mother was home but was in the basement doing laundry."

Kyle took a deep breath and continued, "I had the school nurse check her out. There are three light bruises on her upper left forearm. The nurse took pictures with a Polaroid camera as we have been trained because the bruises could be gone in a few days. As you know, we are mandatory reporters. There is no way I can make this call to the Department of Human Services [DHS]. The superintendent will try to fire me for sure. He can be crazy!"

The principal replied, "Kyle, you know that the only person who can call DHS is the person who interviewed the victim. So they will ask whoever calls if they are the person who talked directly to the victim. They will not continue with the call if the answer is no."

"I know the rules; I've had to make many calls over my twenty-some years as a counselor. However, this is a serious issue with ramifications beyond belief. Linda is a senior and graduating in June. She has had minor issues at school involving friends and teachers. She does have a temper." Kyle was calming down.

"Whatever we decide to do, it will have to be before the day ends, Kyle. So go back to your office and have Linda stay with you until I get back to you."

***

This is a very interesting dilemma. The laws and rules are evident. You are the high school principal.

- What are your next steps?
- Is this a mandatory reporting incident?
- Do you need anyone to help you?
- You know the superintendent has a short fuse, so before the call to DHS is made, who might you contact?
- Is it Kyle's job to decide if Linda is telling the truth?
- Should Linda's mother be contacted?

Scenario 13

Assistant Superintendent

On July 2, Dr. Jocelyn Nesbit and her family were boating on the Mississippi River. As a superintendent finishing her first year, taking a week off was something she looked forward to, especially with her family. As a practice, if a call came through on her cell phone, it wasn't answered unless it was a known number. This time, though, when the phone rang and she didn't recognize the number, she took the call anyway.

"Dr. Nesbit?" Melissa Freeman, one of the district's elementary principals, was in tears, and Dr. Nesbit had trouble understanding her. So she calmed her down and asked what was wrong.

"I received a letter today from Dr. Goodman, assistant superintendent, placing me on an improvement plan. In addition, there are two forms along with a return stamped envelope. He is asking me to sign the forms and send them back. I have never had a meeting with him regarding an improvement plan, which is a total surprise."

The proper protocol for an administrator to be placed on an improvement plan was not to send a letter—it was very involved. "Melissa, please put everything you received in an envelope and put my name on it. Then take it to the administration building, which is open today, and give it to the receptionist. I will alert her that you are coming and ask her to have the custodian open my door and put it on my desk. I know you only have an eleven-month contract and are off until August first, but I will get to the bottom of everything next week. Are you in town next week?"

Still sobbing, Melissa said, "Thank you, Dr. Nesbit. I look forward to meeting with you next week." As Dr. Nesbit hung up, she knew she would be unable to put this out of her mind for the rest of her week off.

***

You are the superintendent. (Hint: There have been times in your first year that you have had some issues with Dr. Goodman.)

- What will your first steps be?
- Who will you talk to?
- Will you involve the school attorney?
- Will you visit with the other assistant superintendent in charge of human resources?
- How serious is this situation?
- Does the board president need to know there is an issue?

Scenario 14

Principal Issues

Dr. Dennis Patterson found that starting a new job as a school superintendent brought some interesting issues. For example, parents with previous complaints and teachers' problems sometimes resurface. While the superintendent found this to be different, in this instance, the parents and teachers brought up alarming issues and rumors regarding the high school principal.

The union president came to Dr. Patterson's office and explained that the high school principal was making inappropriate comments and requests to female teachers. She gave examples, one of which was alarming. The principal asked a math teacher, who was single, if she would pick up his laundry and drop it off at his home in the evening.

The teacher picked it up for the principal but delivered it back to school and hung it on the principal's office doorknob. According to the union president, the principal questioned the teacher, asking why she wouldn't drop it off at his home. The superintendent asked the union president who the teacher was, but she said she had come to her confidently and didn't want to share further.

In Dr. Patterson's opinion, the principal's conduct was inappropriate, but he wanted to honor the teacher's request. A week later, a parent called from her place of business and asked the superintendent for an appointment because the principal had come to her hotel where she was the manager and was inappropriate. She didn't want to talk on the phone. He knew the parent and said he would come to her office that afternoon.

When he arrived at the hotel and went to her office, she was in tears. She explained that the high school principal had a guest clinician coming to town to work with teachers from the district and would need a conference room to work with small groups. She showed him the two conference rooms, and then he asked what the accommodations looked like for bedrooms. As they entered one of the bedrooms, he put his arms around her and pushed her toward the bed.

The manager pushed him back and slapped him, telling him to leave, which he did. She explained that her daughter was very involved with the student council, and the principal was the sponsor of that group. She wasn't sure what to do and didn't want her daughter to know about the incident.

The situation wasn't on school property but was school business.

***

You are the superintendent of this school district. What will you do?

- What are the issues?
- Is more investigation needed?
- What initial decisions will you make?
- Do you contact the school attorney?
- How fast will you act?
- Is this a "her word against the principal" situation?

This is a tough one.

Scenario 15

Bananas

High school speech classes are usually required as one of the English classes needed for graduation. Everyone can remember getting up in front of the class and giving different types of speeches like after-dinner speeches, readings, and demonstration speeches. Students who like to deliver speeches and want to further their skills can take a series of speech classes, usually finishing with Advanced Speech.

As the high school principal in a suburban district, George Swanson knew he had an excellent speech and forensics department headed by Dan Rydel. Dan was one of the best drama coaches and speech instructors in the metro area. His students entered the district, state, and national contests and were quite successful. They also hosted speech contests and had a powerful parent booster organization for the arts. So, at this high school, speech and drama were meaningful and well supported.

Advanced Speech class was predominately a senior class, as students would have had to take Speech I (typically during sophomore year), Speech II, and then Advanced Speech. Dan liked the class—it was a two-semester class, and by the second semester, all the students were doing well and were winning many contests.

The final speeches for the second semester were demonstration speeches, videotaped as part of the students' written and electronic portfolios. Part of the process by this point was for students to peer-edit and critique speeches. In addition, other schools would visit or be sent copies of Dan's curriculum because it was deemed very progressive and influential.

Dan was a very private person, and while many speech and drama instructors were extroverts, Dan was an introvert who put up with very little nonsense in class and on the stage from his students. It was unusual for a right-brained curriculum to have a left-brained instructor, but Dan was always very concrete and sequential. His students would always kid him about being so formal and so strict. They would also miss him as much as any teacher they had when they graduated.

This Advanced Speech class was excellent but also very trying for Dan. He would comment that they had more talent than many in the past, but he also couldn't trust them in some instances to do what was expected and not goof around in his absence. The demonstration speeches were going along just fine until Calvin Ordel, a fine speech student and a leader in the senior class, asked Mr. Rydel if he could do a demonstration speech on the use of condoms since the deadly AIDS crisis was upon them. Calvin said it would be a good speech and maybe it would save a life in the future.

This was the first time Principal Swanson had ever seen Dan shaken up. Dan was asking the principal if he would approve of him allowing the request by Calvin to do a demonstration speech on the use of condoms as a prevention practice for the AIDS virus. Calvin had assured Mr. Rydel that he would not use any props other than a condom and would explain how it was used to prevent sexually transmitted diseases.

In this speech, he would focus on AIDS and explain how it was transmitted and how it could kill an individual. Calvin had also asked each class member (all but one was already eighteen) to sign a release and a permission slip for him to do the speech. In addition, the student under eighteen had secured a written permission slip from her parents.

While Dan was reluctant to allow Calvin to do the speech, he was also aware of the importance of this information and trusted Calvin implicitly. Principal Swanson and Dan both discussed the situation, and finally, Principal Swanson decided to give Dan permission to move ahead. Since it was videotaped, Calvin would have to follow through on his promise, and since everyone in the class did not object, it seemed okay.

That Friday, Calvin was scheduled to give the speech, and Principal Swanson asked Dan if he wanted him to stop in. Dan said he didn't want to draw more attention to this speech than any other. However, if he wanted to watch the tape, he was welcome to after class, and since it was the last hour of the day, Dan would stop in and let him know how it all went.

Dan's account of the speech after school was quite interesting. Calvin had brought a bag up to the front of the room. He had charts showing how the disease broke down a person's immune system when the virus entered the body, and he had a PowerPoint presentation of the current statistics on the AIDS virus. It was quite well done . . . until he got to the end, when he told the class that even though a condom could help protect a person from getting the virus, it wasn't a sure thing, especially if it was not put on correctly. Calvin then took a banana and a condom from the bag. He opened the condom and graphically explained how it was used and put on. Then he put it on the banana to finish his demonstration. Dan said he was without color on his face when this happened in class but thought it would be more of a big deal if he stopped the demonstration, so he let it go. He explained that the students clapped and told Calvin that his speech was the best!

Dan finished by explaining that the student who had run the video camera told him after the speech that she had a problem with the tape and it didn't work, so there was no record of the speech. One of the other students stayed after class to tell Mr. Rydel that this was their class's senior prank on him and that they had paid Calvin $50 to do this speech, knowing that Mr. Rydel would die, which he was doing as he finished telling the story to Principal Swanson.

***

Whew—you are the principal!

- What are the issues?
- What will you do now?
- Will you discipline Calvin?
- Do you inform the superintendent?
- Should you warn the school board?

Scenario 16

Affair

Ms. Sally Whitfield, high school principal, loved attending high school wrestling events, especially weekend tournaments. The team won second place at the large school tournament on Saturday, and she was excited for them. On her way home after stopping for a late lunch, she was passing a motel and noticed the school station wagon parked in the motel's parking lot.

Sally turned around, went back to the motel, and parked next to the vehicle to ensure that it was the district's vehicle. The signage on the car was her district's. The motel had two floors, and all the rooms faced the parking lot. She would have to check with the transportation director Monday about who had checked out the vehicle. Sally got back in her car and drove home.

On Monday morning, Sally stopped by the transportation parking lot and went into the garage. Joey Swartz, the transportation director, saw her come in, smiled, and said, "To what do I owe the pleasure of your visit, Sally?"

"Good to see you, Joey. Who had the school station wagon Saturday?"

Joey didn't have to look it up. "Assistant wrestling coach Al Campbell. Why do you ask?"

"I can't discuss that with you, Joey. Sorry." She thanked him and went to the high school office.

Sally was not sure exactly where to start. What reason would Mr. Campbell have for being at the motel unless he met someone there? The motel was only fifteen miles from her school district. She decided to talk with her assistant principal, Peter Pace.

She went to his office and said, "Good morning, Peter. I hope you had a great weekend."

"Yes, I did. My wife and I went to her parents' home, and I appreciated you covering the wrestling tournament on Saturday so we could go out of town. What's up, Sally?"

She shut the office door and sat down. "On my way back from the wrestling tournament, I saw our school station wagon parked at a motel on Nineteenth Street. Al Campbell checked it out. Do you know anything about why he would be parked there?"

Peter was slow to respond. "There are rumors that Al is having an affair, but they are only rumors."

"Do you know who he is supposedly having an affair with?"

"Only rumors."

"Okay. What are the rumors, Peter? Our school vehicle was parked at a motel, which is unacceptable!"

Peter said, "The rumor is that Al and Julie Harris are involved."

"So we potentially have two high school teachers having an affair. One teaches math and the other physical education."

"That's only a rumor, Sally. I have no proof and have never seen them during the school day demonstrating inappropriate behavior."

***

You are the high school principal.

- What are your next steps?
- Do you inform the superintendent?
- Do you bring in Al Campbell?
- Do you bring in Julie Harris?
- Do you contact the school attorney and ask for help?
- Is this a school district issue?

Scenario 17

Politics

School superintendents receive calls from their principals frequently. Most of the calls are simple questions or making appointments. However, this Friday afternoon, Holden Coring, superintendent, received a call from the elementary principal, Marlis Leary. She sounded alarmed and out of breath.

"Mr. Coring, I need your help. An older man just walked through the lower elementary playground naked! The playground supervisor hollered at the children to come to her, and she took them inside. The police were called, and they took the gentleman into custody. What do you want us to do now?"

Superintendent Coring answered, "Did the police talk with you before they took the man to the police station?"

"Yes. They want to interview the playground supervisor and then talk with me. I have never experienced anything like this. Do you want to be part of this interview?"

The superintendent said he would come over to the elementary school immediately. He knew this would be a juicy story for the newspaper.

When he arrived at the principal's office, the police chief was with the principal and the playground supervisor. The chief took down the account details from the supervisor and the principal. Neither of them knew who the man was or had seen him previously.

Superintendent Coring then asked the chief what the options were for the district. He explained, "You can ask the court for a restraining order so that legally, this person could never be on school property again. We will help the district with this." Superintendent Coring told the chief to start the process.

***

You are the superintendent. What are your next steps?

- Do you call the school board president?
- Do you contact the school attorney?
- Do you instruct the principal to send a letter home describing the incident?
- Do you ask the principal to have the guidance counselor visit the children on the playground?
- Do you write a press release?

PART II

Scenario Solutions

Solution 1

Loaded Gun in Elementary School

As a superintendent, establishing relationships with area leaders, the press, the public, the police, the school board, the newspaper editorial board, and the retired community must happen routinely. You can't just ask them for help only when you need something

After leaving the elementary school, Dr. Curry knew she was on a time crunch. So she first called the school board president, explained everything to her, and said there was no way she could live with recommending expulsion for this third grader under the circumstances.

The board president knew the law and asked how she would resolve everything without the press and parents, making it impossible not to expel the student. Dr. Curry explained that she would go to the newspaper, the NBC affiliate in their city, and the police department. She felt confident that things should work out by the time she met with all of them. Finally, she needed the president to contact each board member with the details and call her if they couldn't support the decision. She said she would start calling immediately.

Her first stop was the NBC affiliate TV station. The longtime evening anchor was in his office, and Dr. Curry had played tennis with his wife and given him some terrific stories to cover in their school system—good and bad.

Dr. Curry started, "We have had a third-grade student bring a loaded gun to school this morning. Here is the letter home to parents. But, there is more to the story you cannot share on the news when I tell you, as it will ruin him for the rest of his life." Then she shared everything.

The news anchor leaned back in his desk chair and said, "Wow, what a touching story. You have my word, Dr. Curry. How will I know the newspaper won't print the entire story when they hear it? Everything leaks out, you know?"

"They are my next stop, and I will say this to them and now to you. If you decide to share the entire story, it will be the last time your station will set foot in our school system for good or bad issues."

He smiled and said, "You have a deal."

Superintendent Curry had a monthly meeting with the editorial board of the well-read local daily newspaper. Her administrative assistant had called them and asked for an emergency meeting. She thanked the board for meeting on short notice, shared everything she had shared with the TV station, and then sat down. Dr. Curry knew this situation would be a tougher pill to swallow for them as they were much more cutthroat than the TV station.

"So can I trust that the only thing you will share is what is in the letter home to parents?"

The editorial board members looked at each other, and the lead editor said, "We will have to discuss this further, and we will let you know."

Curry quickly almost shouted, "That's not acceptable. I have previously been to you sharing inside serious political situations and answered every question you have asked me truthfully. I know this is your paper, and you can do what you want, but a youngster's future is at stake here." She swallowed and continued, "If you decide to share everything, I will personally take out a one-page advertisement and tell the story of how insensitive you are and that you refused to only share what wouldn't ruin this little boy's life, and none of your reporters will ever get onto our school grounds again."

The lead editor said, "Okay. We understand and will only share what is in the letter home."

She smiled, thanked them, and left for the police department.

The police chief and the superintendent were very close. There were six full-time school resource officers in the school district, and the SRO from the elementary school where this took place had shared the entire situation with the chief. The chief said he completely agreed with the plan and to contact him if Dr. Curry needed anything else. The superintendent's blood pressure started to return to normal for the first time since early morning.

Dr. Curry called the school board president, and she said all the board members were on board. Next, she called Maya and shared that the student's previous school principal would love to have him back. They "loved him." Dr. Curry told her she had done a terrific job and was so proud of her. Then, the principal started crying on the phone. Dr. Curry said, "If I were in your office now, I would give you a giant hug, Maya. You are an awesome child advocate."

When she returned to the central office, she had her cabinet come to the conference room and shared everything with them. They all were thrilled with the outcome.

The key to the outcome in this scenario was honest and frequent relationships built over time with community leaders and companies. Finally, the third grader graduated from high school and went to community college, just because you are wondering.

PSEL Standards 2, 3, 5, 6

Solution 2

Drum Line

The band director left the office dejected. The principal told him he would work on the issue and get back to him. The athletic director had been in the district a long time, and Mr. McMillan went to his office and explained the situation.

"Jerry, what do you think about what the band director was told?"

"Mr. McMillan, I stay out of this stuff; everyone has done what they have done forever, and trying to rock the boat isn't my thing."

That told the principal a lot about the athletic director. When Mr. McMillan returned to his office, he told his assistant principal what had happened, and she was neutral. She would support whatever he wanted. However, she didn't like the message from the sponsor to the band director.

The principal scheduled an appointment with the cheerleading sponsor for after school. Ms. Matson was a teacher in the business department and very well respected.

He asked his assistant principal to join them for the meeting. When it began, and before the principal could say a word, Ms. Matson quickly asked, "So what is this meeting about?"

"We understand you told the new band director that his drumline could not perform at the homecoming community/school pep assembly."

"You are new and don't understand that this assembly is a showcase for the community and student body. But, unfortunately, the band has a bad image in the district, and we don't want to ruin the assembly with a crummy drumline performance." She crossed her arms, indicating that she was closed to any conversation.

Fuming, Mr. McMillan responded, "Ms. Matson, the band will play the school song twice, as you informed the band director, and the drumline will perform during the event."

"You can't tell me that they have to play. That is up to me as the sponsor."

"Ms. Matson, you now have a choice. They play, or I will look for a new sponsor."

The assistant principal was sitting a little behind Ms. Matson and smiled quickly.

Mr. McMillan added, "You will inform the band director that you changed your mind and would welcome the drumline's performance."

The cheerleading sponsor looked down at the floor, saying, "I have never been spoken to this way and may file a grievance."

"That is your right, Ms. Matson, but you will tell the band director they will perform, and you will do it when you walk out of my office."

She got up and stormed out of the office.

The assistant principal was excited; no one had ever told this teacher anything like this, and she pretty much did what she wanted as she and the previous principal were close friends outside of school.

Fifteen minutes later, the band director came to the principal's office and said that Ms. Matson had changed her mind and the drumline could perform. He was very thankful. The principal didn't share any information about the meeting.

Two weeks later, the homecoming assembly started. First, the band played the school song while the cheerleaders led the crowd. Next, speeches were given by the head coach, the captain of the football team, the athletic director, and some community leaders. Then the sponsor announced that there would be a special performance by the drumline.

A loud tap on the side of a single snare drum began from the corner away from the main bleachers. Everyone looked toward the entrance. Then, the drumline marched out to each tap in single file. They were dressed in jeans, and all wore sunglasses and school colors. Two members were on the football team and had their jerseys. The line took a sharp left turn and marched to the center of the gym.

The taps stopped, and suddenly, the drumline took off with wild patterns in perfect unison. They were leaning forward, backward, and sideways altogether. Their sticking was in perfect syncopation, and the crowd was on their feet, yelling and clapping with the beat. The drum patterns were astonishing and complex.

Then, after five minutes, they stopped, turned to the right, and marched off to the sound of one tap with every step. The audience wanted more, going crazy as they had never heard anything like this.

Jason McMillan was standing in the corner looking at the crowd and was excited about the drumline and the new director. Since the football team was ranked number one, there were pep assemblies for all home games that fall, and the number one request was that everyone wanted to hear and watch the drumline. They were even asked to perform at various home basketball games.

The cheerleading sponsor never said a word about how well things turned out, and quite honestly, Mr. McMillan didn't care. Doing the right thing bucked tradition in this case and was well worth it. The drumline tradition continues today.

PSEL Standards 1, 2, 3, 5, 6, 7

Solution 3

Motorcycle Ride

Principal Carter's next step was to call Melissa's mother and ask her to come to school. When she arrived, Ms. Becker and the principal explained the entire situation to her and told her that Ms. Becker would like to talk more to Melissa with her mom present. Melissa's mother was a very caring and concerned parent and admitted that Melissa had gone through a difficult summer and acted like a different person. She had entered puberty, her father had moved out of the house, and her best friend had moved out of state, with all these changes leaving her an emotional mess. However, Melissa had told her mom that her favorite teacher was Mr. Aldrich and that he made her feel important again and helped her with social studies.

Ms. Becker and Melissa's mother then left the office together to talk to Melissa. Ned had finished writing his account of the incident and was asked to review it with the principal. It was identical to what he had verbally told him earlier. Mr. Carter explained to Ned that Melissa's mother was with Ms. Becker, and they were going to talk with her and that for now, all he could do was sit tight and wait.

Ned asked, "If this is her word against mine and she stays with her story, I am finished as a teacher forever, aren't I?" The principal again reiterated that he just needed to wait and that nothing more could be done until Ms. Becker and Melissa's mom finished talking to Melissa. He asked why his question wasn't answered and was told it was too premature to discuss.

However, Mr. Carter knew that clearly this had the potential of causing Ned severe problems as a teacher. On Saturday, he had placed himself in a situation with Melissa that had all the earmarking of severe consequences.

By 2:00 p.m., Ms. Becker and Melissa's mother decided that Melissa would go home with her mom. Melissa's mom wanted some time with her daughter to talk to her about the alleged incident. Melissa's mom remarked that she questioned the accuracy of Melissa's story because she believed that Melissa would have told her about what happened before she would have come to school and told Ms. Becker.

However, during the rest of the afternoon and evening, Melissa did not change her story; she cried a lot. Later that evening, Melissa's mother called Ms. Becker to ask if she and Melissa could come in the following day so all three could talk some more. They arrived at 8:00 a.m. and went to the guidance office.

Knowing that Melissa had not yet changed her story, Ned was very concerned as he walked down the hallway to teach his first-hour class. Ms. Becker and Principal Carter had decided that if Melissa had not changed her story by noon, they would have to contact the school attorney.

At 11:15 a.m., Ms. Becker came to Mr. Carter's office and asked to have Ned come to the guidance office to meet with Melissa and her mom. Melissa had something to say but would not tell anyone unless Mr. Aldrich was present. So Mr. Aldrich was summoned from his class-room and went to the guidance office. In tears, Melissa explained that at the Friday night football game, she saw Mr. Aldrich with his girlfriend and that it broke her heart since she had a massive crush on him, and she was sure he felt the same way about her.

When she saw him Saturday morning leaving his apartment, and he asked her if she wanted a ride on his motorcycle, she was excited. When she held on to him as they rode, she felt terrific. When nothing more happened at school when he showed her the construction site, got his work from his classroom, and then took her home, she was crushed and jealous of his girlfriend. She decided to hurt him by making up a story she knew would get him in trouble.

Ms. Becker explained to Melissa that sometimes people make very serious mistakes and that these mistakes can hurt others for the rest of their lives. However, if someone has the opportunity to correct these mistakes before they cause permanent damage, then often, things can change back to the way they were. Melissa wanted Mr. Aldrich to be her friend even though she had lied and tried to get him in trouble.

Mr. Carter and the counselor decided that Melissa needed to be with her mom for the rest of the day. Her mom was going to take her to their family physician to get the name of a professional counselor for Melissa. Later that afternoon, Melissa's mom called and said she felt it would be best for Melissa to have a different social studies teacher, which was quickly arranged.

Ned, of course, was relieved. The whole incident was documented so that if anyone questioned what had happened, there was a formal accounting of everything in the future. In the write-up, there was a clause warning Ned that he should not give students rides on his motorcycle or in his car in the future. This was a grave mistake, and while his actions were well intended, he used very poor judgment, which could have cost him his teaching license. Ned is still teaching today and is considered an outstanding social studies teacher.

Melissa did not tell this story to anyone again. She finished middle school and did quite well in high school. Ms. Becker had done an excellent job working with Melissa and her mother, which helped save Mr. Aldrich's career and a lot of embarrassment. Melissa's mother deserved much of the credit. She understood her daughter well enough to spend time with her and keep talking about the situation before making a formal accusation and going to the police as she could have.

Later, this story was shared with aspiring teachers as they started their practicum. Most of them were squirming in their seats as the story was told. A number of them have explained later that they were in a situation where they could have given a student a ride somewhere and remembered the story and either found another adult to go with them or another way for the student to get where they needed to go. But, unfortunately, when dealing with young students, sometimes things that seem pretty harmless, no matter how well intended, can create severe issues if the possible consequences are not well thought out.

PSEL Standards 2, 5, 6, 8

Arena Conferences
Missing Teacher

Since the assistant principal was suspicious of Ms. Wheeler's story, Dr. Ford brought in the department chair and visited with her, sharing what information he had.

He asked, "Has Ms. Wheeler missed conferences previously?"

"In my twenty years as department chair, she has been here ten of those years and has missed five conferences. The previous principal dealt with her, so I don't know what came of those meetings."

He thanked her, and she left the office. The principal and assistant continued to discuss strategy. Without factual information, they agreed it would be their word against hers. The assistant principal asked, "So, what is our next move?"

"I will contact the police department and ask about any accidents at that intersection on the date and time that Ms. Wheeler had shared." So the call was made, and the officer was given the date and times to check.

"Let's see," the officer said, looking through the records. "No, there was no accident at that location on that date and time. What was the name of the person supposedly in the accident?"

Dr. Ford gave him her name, and there was no accident record with that name. Thanking the officer for his trouble, Dr. Ford then contacted Human Resources and explained the whole ordeal. The HR director permitted Dr. Ford to suspend Ms. Wheeler for three days without pay and sent over the form she would have to sign. The assistant principal scheduled a conference with Ms. Wheeler right after school.

Ms. Wheeler came into the office at the designated time with the assistant principal.

Dr. Ford started, "Ms. Wheeler. Please share again why you were absent from parent-teacher conferences."

She fired back, "I already told you. So why are you asking again?"

"I wanted to allow you an opportunity to change your story. Since that is what you are staying with, you will be receiving a three-day suspension without pay. I have a report from the police department, and there was no accident at that intersection or anywhere involving your name."

She sat back and said, "I just didn't feel good, and since I have missed previous conferences, I didn't think you would believe me."

"You are correct about us not believing you, Ms. Wheeler."

"I will be filing a grievance on your decision, and I know if it gets to the school board, they will support me as they have in the past. However, you are new and just don't get it!"

Dr. Ford responded, "I get it, Ms. Wheeler. You are a liar and have been very unprofessional."

The form was reviewed for her to sign, and he ensured that she understood it. She didn't have to agree but did have to sign, which she refused to do. The assistant principal was asked to witness that she refused to sign and put her initials by the signature line.

The last sentence stated, "Further discipline up to and including a termination recommendation will occur if this behavior continues." Ms. Wheeler was furious, took the initialed form, and stomped out of the office.

Dr. Ford knew she would complain to any faculty member she could find on the way out of the building, which was okay with him. Finally, her department head stopped by and said she told her everything before leaving and was totally out of control. "It's about time someone held her accountable. Thank you."

Doing the right thing, in this case, was pretty easy. But unfortunately, the previous principal had ignored the behavior of Ms. Wheeler and other faculty members, which only allowed more folks to act in unacceptable ways.

Looking the other way never works. When your faculty knows you will not do this, it helps everyone be more accountable.

By the way, the grievance went no further as the union president told her they would not support any grievance in this situation.

PSEL Standards 1, 2, 4, 5, 6, 7, 8, 9

Solution 5

Newspaper Conflict

Dr. Martin's next meeting with the editorial board was the week after the article about the two students getting arrested for possession of drugs in the high school with the intent to distribute. She clipped out the article from the neighboring district and put it in a separate folder, and saved the front-page article containing her high school students' arrest in another folder.

Her director of communications always came with her to the editorial board meetings. Dr. Martin asked her not to be surprised by what she would say and do. After the standard greetings at the start of the meeting, the newspaper's editor in chief, Gene, asked if there were any updates on the current construction projects.

Dr. Martin responded, "Gene. Before we start, I am troubled with the front-page coverage you gave to the two students arrested for possession of drugs with intent to deliver." She knew Gene would take the offensive right away.

"Dr. Martin, what we print and where we print it is not anything you can or will control."

She said quickly, "I agree and don't want any part in those decisions. That's not my problem. The problem is how you cover our neighboring school district differently than ours."

"I take offense to that." Gene was now visibly irritated. "We don't cover them differently."

She took out the edition's front page containing her school's story, opened her folder, and laid the tiny article on page 16 next to hers. "Please tell me your definition of equal treatment and add bias to that when you answer. These articles are only a few months apart with the same scenarios."

Gene looked at them both and responded, "I will have our reporters and editorial team get together, and I will get back to you, Dr. Martin."

"I don't want you to meet with anyone and get back to me. Your paper treats our impoverished high school differently from our neighbors to the west, and you know it. If anything like this happens again, I promise you and your reporters that they will never be permitted to set foot in any of our schools. We will give you nothing, good or bad." She closed her folders and told her communications director that they were leaving.

Dr. Martin had cleared this with her school board president, who was equally upset and supportive of what would be presented to the editorial board. When she reviewed the editorial meeting with her, she was pleased.

Gene contacted her administrative assistant two weeks later and asked for an appointment. The only thing he could say when they met was that she was right—there had been different metrics for covering the two districts, and that would not happen again. He continued, "All of our staff met, and the two articles you pointed out were presented." Again, Gene promised her that nothing like this would happen again.

She thanked him, and he left.

Doing the right thing sometimes means being direct and firm. Her district held a winning hand in this case, and the editor knew it. The trend to treat the communities differently had been going on for years before Cassie Martin was hired. So when she saw the two considerable discrepancies in the articles, she knew it was time to call and question it.

PSEL Standards 1, 2, 3, 4

Solution 6

Parent Demand

Here is how Dr. Cassidy responded:

"Okay—let me write up an agreement for you to sign. It will state that you want your son to be treated differently than any other student because you were Citizen of the Year, donated computers, are a prominent attorney, and rode in the first float at the July Fourth parade. I'll approve it right after you sign it."

Mr. Guzzy frowned, smiled, and said, "I can't sign that."

Dr. Cassidy responded, "And I can't approve your request."

"Thank you for your time, Dr. Cassidy. It was good to meet you."

Cassidy knew that Mr. Guzzy would never sign the request, and he also hoped that by reading the request, Mr. Guzzy would recognize that he was really out of line. Later they became pretty good friends, and Mr. Guzzy continued to volunteer and was on some of the high school committees.

Doing the right thing sometimes requires a quick seat-of-the-pants decision!

PSEL Standards 1, 3, 5, 8, 9

Solution 7

Marching Band Sousaphones

Dr. Hicks had experienced similar issues of one school getting something and the other not. It always made things murky; in this case, the west side high school band boosters wanted equal treatment.

The west side principal and Dr. Hicks met to discuss everything. She understood why he made the decision and explained that this booster group was very powerful and influential. They were willing to do anything for their band program, including making things very political if needed, as they had in the past. She planned on attending the meeting with Dr. Hicks.

Next, Dr. Hicks met with his school board president—only to make him aware of the situation, not to ask him if what he did was appropriate. The board president gave him some information regarding who some of the booster members were and what their positions were in the community. This helped him since he would see these folks in places other than the booster meeting. The board president added that this group was very powerful and influential.

Mason thought about asking the assistant superintendent in charge of equity to attend the meeting, but after talking with her and explaining what he was going to say, she thought the meeting would go just fine.

The booster meeting started at 6:00 p.m., and Dr. Hicks was first on the agenda. Band booster president Janice Willows introduced him and gave them the information regarding the east side band program receiving $12,000 for marching sousaphones. She said the west side program had not received the same amount and gave him the microphone.

"Good evening, and thank you for inviting me to your meeting. I have known about your outstanding marching band program for many years and saw them at the Valley Fest Contest in West Des Moines a few years ago. You all should be proud of your program."

"I looked up your fundraising receipts for the past five years. Your average for each of the fundraisers was about $17,000. I looked up the same for the east side band boosters, and their average for the past five years was about $3,000 for each fundraiser. So there is no question a discrepancy exists between the two schools' abilities to raise needed funds."

"That doesn't make any difference, sir," one parent yelled. "If the district can give one program $12,000, it has to give the other the same amount." A few people clapped.

Dr. Hicks smiled and continued, "Let's discuss the difference between equal and equitable. Equal means that both are treated the same. Equitable considers the differences so that there is some equality in the end. So I have a proposal. If you combine your band booster club with the east side booster club and have a district-wide band booster club, you all can determine the needs of both programs and act accordingly."

You could have heard a pin drop, and no one said a word to anyone for a while. Then, finally, Janice Willows stood up, saying, "Well, we will consider this proposal, Dr. Hicks, and get back to you with our decision. Thank you for coming. Let's take a short break."

He walked out with the west side principal, and she said, "Awesome move. They never saw that coming. So it will be interesting to hear their answer."

The following week, Ms. Willows called Dr. Hicks, saying, "We have decided not to look into combining booster clubs and will drop our request for the $12,000. Thank you for speaking at our meeting."

Dr. Hicks knew they would never combine forces with the other booster club, and maybe they learned the differences between equality and equity. The educational reporter from the local daily paper heard about the meeting and called Dr. Hicks. After the superintendent explained everything to him, he laughed and said, "Awesome." But fortunately, it never made the paper.

Doing what is right in this case was very political and, in Dr. Mason Hicks's mind, came out perfectly.

PSEL Standards 1, 3, 5, 8, 10

Solution 8

Closing an Elementary School

The following two school board meetings each had about forty people speaking for no more than five minutes regarding the proposed closure of the elementary school. No one spoke in support of the proposal. Before the scheduled board meeting, where the issue was on the agenda with a recommendation for closure, Dr. Mason talked with the board president and asked her what she thought.

"Dr. Mason, I know this is the right thing to do, but I have to live in this community. As an African American, I understand exactly where the community is coming from. So if the board vote comes to me tied on our seven-member school board, I will vote yes. If my vote doesn't change anything, I will vote no. I hope you understand."

They talked for quite a while, and Dr. Mason told her she understood her position. She also explained that she thought the vote would be 5–2 in support and that she need not worry. The board president smiled and said, "Thanks."

The final vote was 5–2 in favor of closing the elementary school. All the school board meetings were on television with a live feed from the NBC affiliate, so the community didn't have to attend to see the discussion. Some did, but only about thirty. The daily newspaper printed the decision as the headline the next day but didn't take a position.

The week after the board decision, the district was contacted by the Office of Civil Rights (OCR) out of Chicago and was served with a notice claiming discrimination. The notice outlined what the allegations were but not who filed them. Dr. Mason learned that the OCR had a practice never to reveal who filed a complaint. The OCR outlined all the data that they expected to be ready when they visited with their team. The team would spend three days interviewing school district employees, board members, facilities committee members, and the community. Since all three OCR members were attorneys, the district's attorney recommended that she be present for all interviews.

Dr. Mason and her team prepared five three-ringed four-inch notebooks with the requested data. The OCR interviews were neutral; they were just collecting data. It was an interesting experience. (What is very interesting is that the case is still open today. The claim that the children would suffer academically was top of the OCR's issue. It is open, and they didn't pursue it because of what the district did with all the students who moved to three other schools.)

The district transported all the elementary students from the closed school, where before they had to walk to school. They flagged each student to establish academic, discipline, and attendance baselines. After the first year, the group was pulled together like they were still at their old school. Academics were up, discipline referrals were down, and attendance improved by 26 percent. The district sent this to the OCR, and the data showed no academic decline for the next two years. In fact, their academics improved. Unfortunately, the OCR never responded to the reports.

Doing the right thing is hard, but it's always right. This was a very emotional roller coaster for the district, but it was the right thing to do. The school district would have been challenged more than usual on future issues if they had not made the recommendation after all the data had been collected and public meetings had been held.

The new superintendent was very happy not to have to deal with this issue!

PSEL Standards 1, 3, 4, 5, 8, 9, 10

Solution 9

Receptionist and Maintenance Assistant

After Sherry left the office, Dr. Williams and Dr. Johnston started game-planning what was next. But first, they called the school attorney. Dr. Johnston started the phone conversation. "So you are on speakerphone with Dr. Williams and me." They explained everything they knew to that point.

The school attorney, Calin, was terrific and offered suggestions. "One thing we can do is get Kenny to share what he was doing on Sunday with the receptionist. Then we can tell him what the receptionist's version was. Then see what happens. Have Dr. Williams take notes or record the session with Kenny's permission. Then call me if you need more help. Since he is one of her supervisors, the relationship, consensual or not, is not acceptable." The call ended.

Dr. Johnston said to Dr. Williams, "One thing I know is that Kenny likes to gamble. He used to go to the casino about twenty miles away with the former superintendent so they could be somewhat anonymous. So that gives me an idea. Do we have a formal notification of intent to retire form?"

"Yes, we do."

"Make one out using Kenny's name and include the retirement bonus he will receive since he has over twenty years of service. How much would that be?"

Dr. Williams said, "The retirement amount for administrators and supervisors with twenty-some years is about $22,000. I can check for sure."

"Okay. Draw up the regular intent to retire form and make it effective a month from now."

"Do you think you can talk him into retiring?"

"I know it is a long shot, but do you think he wants to gamble on losing $22,000 if he gets fired?"

She laughed, saying, "I have never been through something like this, Dr. Johnston."

"Me neither!"

Knowing that Kenny had deep ties to many folks in the school system, Dr. Johnston contacted the board president and explained that there was a problem with Kenny and that if she heard anything, not to worry. Dr. Johnston didn't tell her any details, in case the board would have to become involved. She thanked him but was worried about his power in the community.

A meeting with Kenny was scheduled for Monday at 10:00 a.m. Dr. Williams and Dr. Johnston met at 9:00 a.m. to go over everything and review the forms. One form was for Kenny to sign that he had had no affair with the receptionist and wanted a formal investigation; the other was the request for retirement. Dr. Williams was very nervous about the meeting, as was Dr. Johnston!

Kenny came in at 10:00 a.m. and sat down with Dr. Williams and the superintendent. "So, what's up?" He was always to the point and seemed very nervous.

Dr. Johnston started, "Kenny, this will not be an easy conversation. A central office employee you supervise has accused you of having a consensual affair, which is a serious problem. Therefore, we would like to record this meeting with your permission."

He agreed and stated, "If this is regarding Sherry, the receptionist, I have been trying to help her through some difficult family problems, nothing else." He leaned back in his chair.

"Kenny, that isn't what her story is, including a promise to leave your wife and marry her."

"She is lying."

"On Sunday morning, the weekend before last, you entered the central office as did Sherry. She says you met in the upstairs women's lounge."

"That is correct. She had called me, troubled, and needed to see me as soon as possible in the upstairs lounge. So I met her there; we talked and then left at separate times."

"Her story differs as she said that she and you had sex in the lounge, and then you said the relationship was over."

"I'm telling you both. She is crazy. No way that happened. This is my word against hers, and this just stinks."

Dr. Johnston said, "Kenny. You have two options, and I want you to listen carefully. Option number one is for the district to do a thorough investigation, including reviewing all your district cell phone records and Sherry's. Also, since a pair of women's underwear was left in that upstairs bathroom that Sunday morning after you met, we will have it tested for DNA. Finally, if her accusations are proven, you will lose your job and not receive your administrative retirement bonus.

"Option number two. Here is a request for retirement effective one month from today, including your retirement bonus of $22,000. If you decide you want a comprehensive investigation to clear your name, we will do that in hopes that you are cleared. It is your call, Kenny."

"How long do I have to make this decision?"

"If you don't want to tell us which option you want, we will start the investigation immediately, which I'm sure you would want us to do when you leave this office."

"So I don't have a chance to talk with my lawyer?"

"Of course, you can talk to your lawyer. These options are your choice, Kenny. I'm sure you would want a complete investigation unless her accusations are factual."

Dr. Johnston knew he had Kenny in a box and would sign the retirement forms as a gambler, knowing he had a ton to lose. Dr. Johnston added, "If you take the retirement option, you cannot talk to Sherry again about anything. Is that clear?"

Kenny leaned forward, picked up the pen, and signed the retirement form, which they knew he would do. Dr. Johnston had heard all the rumors about him and Sherry, and until she came forward, they were only unfounded rumors.

"What are you going to tell everyone about my retirement?"

"That is up to you, Kenny. We will just say you are retiring, nothing else."

They gave Kenny a copy of the signed form, and he left. Dr. Williams said she had never seen anything like it; it was all very legal. They both relaxed, and Dr. Williams said she would talk with Sherry and help her. Two months later, Sherry left for another job in another state.

Doing an investigation with their information would have been one person's word against the other. There was no guarantee of any DNA on the underwear besides Sherry's. So talking together on the phone would not be more than Kenny trying to help her, in Dr. Johnston's opinion.

In this case, doing the right thing was removing Kenny from his position after more than twenty years of service to the district without a potential public mess. When Dr. Johnston was a university professor teaching potential principals and superintendents, he always said there were two ways you could lose your job quickly—"the honey and the money." Either one would be a fatal error.

PSEL Standards 2, 6, 9, 10

Solution 10

Flag Girls

Sam Cook was put in a tough spot by the superintendent. He knew these parents were very influential in the community, or the superintendent wouldn't have come to his home. The conversation continued.

"I have one question for you, Superintendent Langford. What would the coach say if the quarterback on the football team came to the varsity coach and asked to miss Friday's game so he could go to another school's homecoming?"

"That's totally a different scenario, and you know it."

"If you ask the band director if it is different, he would disagree. The girls and their parents made a choice knowing what would happen, and they even signed a contract. So I will do what you are asking on one condition. Ask the head football coach if the quarterback said he would miss the game to go to another football game, and if he did it, would he still be the quarterback the next week? If the coach says he would be, I'll do it."

"You are mixing apples and oranges. I'm sorry you feel that way. I'm placing this on the board agenda next Monday, and I expect you to be there, and I know the parents will be there." Then the superintendent left.

Mr. Cook told the band director not to worry and that he would take all the heat for the situation. He also asked him to attend the Monday meeting with him. The press would be there as anytime there is controversy, it is newsworthy.

The Monday board meeting started at 7:00 p.m., and the flag team contract was on the agenda. When it was time for that agenda item to be discussed, the board president looked over to the superintendent and asked, "Why is this on the agenda? The parents and students all signed a

73

valid agreement and clearly knew that. The parents aren't here, and the flag team members who were dropped aren't present. The only way we will begin to build the arts programs is to support them."

The board president looked at the band director and principal and asked if they had any comments. Both said no. Then the board president asked the board if they had any comments, and they all signaled no. Finally, the board president directed the superintendent not to bring frivolous issues like that to the board.

Mr. Cook felt terrible for the superintendent when none of the parents or kids showed up, as he knew he expected them to come and support his position.

Being new to a job is tough. Doing the right thing sometimes is tough, but it is always right.

PSEL Standards 1, 2, 3, 5, 6, 8

Solution 11

Bus Driver

Dr. Murry jumped in his SUV and drove five minutes to the elementary school. He had called the police chief and met him there as well. The transportation director and another driver were waiting in the parking lot. Dr. Murry told them that he and the chief would speak to Harold. The kids had not yet come out of the building for the field trip.

"Hi, Harold. I need you to turn off the bus and come down the stairs. We have to talk about something." Harold was compliant, and they walked together to Dr. Murry's SUV, not the police car. He didn't want to alarm him any more than he already was.

"We have a concern about some rumors about you, Harold. I would like you to go with the police chief, and I will meet you at the station, and we can sort this out." Harold didn't say anything and just got into the police car. The substitute driver got on the bus, and Harold and the superintendent went to the police station.

At the police station, Dr. Murry explained, "Harold, we have been told that you live in your station wagon now and have a gun. Is this true?"

Harold hung his head and said he lived in his vehicle but did not have a gun. The chief was concerned and asked if it would be okay for him to search his vehicle. He agreed, and they all drove to the bus barn where Harold's vehicle was parked. The search revealed no weapons of any kind.

They thanked the chief and went into the bus barn office. "Harold, I am concerned that your state of mind is pretty frazzled, and I am placing you on a suspension with pay until we can sort things out." Harold left without responding.

Dr. Murry went back to his office and called the school attorney. She was excellent and advised that the driver should not be driving routes for the remainder of the year and to pay him his average monthly amount listed in his contract. The contract would expire, and the district wouldn't issue him another one. He was classified as an at-will employee. Dr. Murry told the transportation director and board members what the attorney had advised.

Two weeks later, the transportation director issued Harold a contract and had him sign it for driving the summer varsity baseball team. Dr. Murry couldn't believe it. The director thought it was okay to drive the team, just not the daily bus routes. But, since he signed it, the school attorney said to pay him another lump sum for the baseball contract and find another driver. Dr. Murry was upset with the transportation director, who said he felt sorry for everything Harold was going through.

Harold would never be reissued any contracts. He was then involved in one of the worst mass murders in Iowa's history.

Here is the AP story. Harold is currently in prison for life.

June 14, 1993

NORWALK, Iowa (AP) _ Neighbors watched as a couple's marriage began falling apart after one of their children died in an accident. Three years later, they watched authorities investigate a shooting that left six dead and one wounded.

Dr. Murry shuddered every time he thought of what could have happened if the district wouldn't have removed Harold from his bus driving duties. Doing the right thing was challenging, because everyone knew that Harold was suffering.

To this day, one thing that Dr. Murry can see in his mind is four open caskets lined up in a row at a church ceremony. Hopefully, none of you reading this scenario will ever have to go through anything like this.

PSEL Standards 2, 3, 5, 6, 8

Solution 12

Superintendent's Daughter

Principal Carver knew that this situation had nowhere to go but down. Linda's case needed to be dealt with just like any reported situation of physical harm to a student. So he contacted the assistant principal, Jeannie, whom he trusted, and asked her to come to his office. She was there in five minutes.

She knew something was serious and sat down, saying, "What's the problem, Henry?"

Mr. Carver explained everything, and Jeannie just slumped in her chair, knowing that things would erupt quickly. She said, "Linda's relationship with her father is terrible. They verbally fight all the time, and her mother is the person who settles things down. This doesn't surprise me at all. . . . But as mandatory reporters, our counselor has to make the call, Henry."

She continued, "Let's call our attorney and run things by him. I want to see the pictures."

The attorney was extremely helpful. He explained, "It depends on the injury and if it would be visible twenty-four hours later. If not, then it is not a mandatory reporting incident. I will fax you the section that applies. Call me back if you need more help."

That section in the questions and answers section from DHS says, "The Iowa DHS uses a definition of 'injury' that requires that evidence of the injury must still exist twenty-four hours after the abuse occurs. Thus, a mark that disappears within the twenty-four hours would not be an 'injury' and thus not reportable."

"Well, that is something neither of us knew." Mr. Carver sure didn't. Kyle gave them the pictures; the bruises were light brown and probably would be gone by morning. So they decided to make this a learning experience for the superintendent and Linda.

Mr. Carver and Jeannie called the superintendent and had him come to Mr. Carver's office. They explained everything and said that if by morning, the bruises were not visible, the counselor would not make the call to DHS. However, the mandatory call would be made if they were still visible. They also called the superintendent's wife to come to the office and shared everything with her, showing her the pictures. Then Mr. Carver went to Kyle's office, where Linda was, and explained everything to her. Linda seemed okay and had calmed down quite a bit.

Mr. Carver returned to his office, where Jeannie was still talking with the superintendent and his wife. Finally, the decision was made that the family needed family counseling. According to Linda, mom, and dad, things were mainly unsettled. So the principal asked Linda to come to his office and meet with all of them.

Linda was relieved that something was going to take place to hopefully help them all get along better. The superintendent was embarrassed that everyone was discussing the situation with him. The team could see that he was irritated even though he had agreed to family counseling. Finally, everyone decided that Linda and the family should go home and arrange family counseling.

After they left, Jeannie and Mr. Carver talked about everything. They were both glad that the attorney had given them advice, and in the morning, Kyle and the school nurse would retake pictures.

The following day, Linda entered the guidance office, and the nurse examined her and took pictures. The bruises were not visible, and Linda went to class. This was reported to her mom and dad to make it official.

The family had scheduled counseling starting the following week. So what began as a potential disaster for the superintendent turned into something that ended up being healthy for the family.

Attorneys cost money, but they are invaluable. Never think that calling them when you need advice is wrong or makes you look weak. You are better off with sound legal advice than stumbling and making poor decisions. If Kyle had made the call to DHS, they would have advised him to wait twenty-four hours. In this case, decisions were made to get the family some much-needed help.

PSEL Standards 2, 5, 6, 8

Solution 13

Assistant Superintendent

The same day that Dr. Nesbit received the call from the principal, she went into overdrive, trying to think of precisely what she was going to do. Her husband asked her about the call as he could see she was upset, and she told him it was business and she couldn't share it with him. He reminded her that they had the remainder of their vacation left and to "chill out!" He was right.

When she returned home, she sat in her home office and started to process the next steps. In her mind, Dr. Goodman had clearly made a terrible decision. He hadn't followed any "plans for assistance protocol," and sending the letter to the principal via USPS mail was a drastic mistake. So she called her other assistant superintendent and told her they needed to talk at 9:00 a.m.

Dr. Nesbit got to her office at 8:00 a.m. and reviewed everything, and at nine, she met Dr. Williams, one of her favorite team members. She was brilliant and not afraid to speak the truth to power. Dr. Williams asked, "Good morning, what's up?"

"You would never believe what Dr. Goodman has done. According to Melissa Freeman, he sent a letter in the mail to her, placing her on a plan of assistance without any previous meetings." Dr. Williams sat back and was shocked.

"He knows better than that. He has been through extensive training regarding the process for placing teachers and administrators on plans of assistance. If Melissa does have difficulties, this will erase everything before July first. She probably would also have a harassment case. This really is a terrible situation."

"I agree. We first need to cover the district legally, call our attorney quickly, and run this by her." Dr. Williams agreed, and they made the call.

Their attorney listened to the entire situation from what Melissa had shared, and they sent the attorney copies that were mailed to her. "I would like you both to be present with any conversations with Melissa and Dr. Goodman from this minute forward. I think the first thing should be bringing in Melissa and having her share everything that has taken place between her and Dr. Goodman from her perspective. Don't agree that there have been any mistakes or pass any judgment on Dr. Goodman during this meeting. After the meeting, call me, and let's make a plan to interview Dr. Goodman. If everything she shared is accurate, we may have some legal exposure. Any questions?"

They both thanked her and didn't have any further questions. Then, Dr. Nesbit contacted Melissa and asked her if she was available that day. She said she could come to her office at 1:00 p.m. Then, Dr. Williams and Dr. Nesbit planned how they would proceed. They agreed that Dr. Williams would be the note taker, and Dr. Nesbit would be the one asking questions. Dr. Williams could, of course, ask questions also, but they needed an accurate record of the meeting.

At 1:00 p.m., Melissa came into the office. Dr. Nesbit started, "Melissa, we would like you to review your evaluation meetings with Dr. Goodman over the last school year to your best recollection."

She said, "Sure, but am I in trouble and possibly going to lose my job? This is really a stressful situation. I haven't slept for many nights since I received the letter."

"We know this is stressful. So we just want you to review the past year, highlighting evaluation meetings with Dr. Goodman."

Melissa started at the beginning of the year by outlining the first meeting with all the principals on cycle for evaluation. Next, Dr. Nesbit outlined everything that would take place during the school year. They all understood that there would be monthly meetings and that the approved goals had to have written action plans to achieve them. These targets would be reviewed monthly.

"There were two targets I didn't meet by January first, but the rest I did. We didn't meet for three months as Dr. Goodman canceled them due to conflicts, but they were never rescheduled. I emailed Dr.

Goodman evidence that I was meeting the two unmet goals. He never responded."

She continued, "Then, in April, we met, and he said I was meeting one of the two goals but not the other. He explained that not meeting one goal would not be too serious but might require me to be on cycle for a second year in a row. I told him that I understood. That was the last time we met. The way he talked to me made me feel that nothing I was doing was good. His attitude toward me was negative, in my opinion."

Dr. Nesbit asked, "Did he ever talk to you about being placed on an improvement plan?"

"No, never."

"Okay, Melissa. Please let us investigate this situation. It would be best if you didn't share anything with anyone about what is happening. I know you are concerned, but trust me when I say I will look into this and get back to you."

She answered, "Thank you, and I understand." Then she left.

Dr. Williams looked up from her notes and said, "You just can't make this stuff up! If everything she shared is only half-true, we have a problem. Let's schedule Dr. Goodman for tomorrow morning." She left, and the superintendent had her administrative assistant schedule Dr. Goodman for 9:00 a.m. the following day

At nine the next day, they sat down with Dr. Goodman. Dr. Nesbit said, "Dr. Goodman, I understand you placed Melissa Freeman on an improvement plan. Is that correct?"

"Yes," he answered. "She hasn't met her targets for the year, which warrants an improvement plan."

"How did the conference go with Melissa when you placed her on an improvement plan?" She was anxious to hear his response, as was Dr. Williams.

"Well, we ran out of time, and I just sent her a notice asking her to sign it and return it to me, which she hasn't done yet."

"Is this the notice you sent her?" She handed him the two notices unsigned.

"Yes, those are the notices. Why do you have them?"

"Dr. Goodman, you don't understand that this is unacceptable. You must follow protocols when placing an employee on an improvement plan. You didn't meet with her each month, and you did not meet with her in person to discuss an improvement plan. Instead, you chose to mail the forms to her, which we find totally unacceptable. How do you think any principal would feel receiving these forms in the mail without an in-person meeting?" Dr. Nesbit was showing her anger.

Goodman did not answer the question. Instead, he just sat there looking at them. Then, finally, he responded, "I didn't think much about how she felt. I just wanted to get the forms to her so she would know she would be on a plan of assistance."

Dr. Nesbit looked at Dr. Williams in amazement that Dr. Goodman had no clue that he had done something wrong and was okay with what he had done. "For your information, Dr. Goodman, she will not be placed on an improvement plan, and you will no longer be her immediate supervisor. We will be lucky that she doesn't accuse you of discrimination or sue the district. Furthermore, I know you have responsibility for evaluating all twenty-one principals, each on a three-year cycle. So that would be seven each year. I am taking that responsibility away from you and reassigning it to three central office administrators, including myself."

Dr. Goodman responded, "That isn't fair. What will all the administrators feel about me, and what will they be told?"

"When we make this official at the August first district administrators meeting, it will be presented so that you can concentrate on curriculum and instruction. You have excellent skills in those areas but not in administrative evaluation. I am also placing a formal disciplinary letter in your file that I will have you sign next week."

Dr. Goodman was somewhat obstinate. "This seems extreme, using just one instance."

"Let me further explain your situation since you still don't understand the ramifications of what you did with Ms. Freeman. Get your resume up to date and start looking for other employment. During this last school year, you have been resentful of not being selected as superintendent, and you have gone out of your way to make that known for at least the last six months. So now you can get things ready to do a nationwide search for a new job. We are done here." The meeting was over

Dr. Goodman got up and left. Dr. Williams was excited to see him not evaluating principals, because she had received minor complaints for years. "This will send a great message to all our principals and central office staff. No one would have expected what you just did, and everyone will silently cheer. But then, they all will start sharpening their pencils, trying to do a better job."

"I remember Jim Collins's book *Good to Great*, where he says it is important to get the right folks in a business on the bus and, more importantly, in the right seat. But, unfortunately, I don't think Dr. Goodman is even the right person to be on the bus." Dr. Nesbit was firm in her statement.

They did a conference call with the attorney and shared everything. She was delighted and added that they needed to meet with Melissa and change her current evaluation status.

Four central office administrators, including the superintendent, were given principal evaluation responsibilities. Dr. Nesbit took the two high school principals, two middle school principals, and Melissa Freeman. She met with Melissa and told her she would review everything she had worked on with her evaluation targets and go from there. Melissa was relieved.

Dr. Goodman was hired as a superintendent in another state in November, which happened to be looking for a candidate focusing on curriculum and instruction.

In summary, it is critical to treat administrators not doing their jobs as just as important as teachers not doing their jobs. According to the district's annual survey, morale went way up for the district. Relationships and accountability are critical for leaders to display.

PSEL Standards 1, 2, 3, 6, 7, 9, 10

Solution 14

Principal Issues

Dr. Patterson knew he had to confront the principal but wanted to talk with the school attorney before that meeting. The attorney was terrific and explained that he needed to visit with the principal. They discussed action and contingency plans depending on what the principal said during the conference. Based on what he knew at this point, Dr. Patterson believed he would be defensive and in denial.

The meeting was scheduled at the end of the following school day. Dr. Patterson started the discussion. "Justin, what can you tell me about asking a teacher to pick up your laundry and deliver it to your home?" Justin was seated at his desk and leaned forward.

"When I arrived here in August, my family had not arrived yet, and I had dropped off items at the cleaners. So I asked a teacher if she minded picking up my laundry and dropping it off at my home. She dropped it off at my office instead. That's all there is to it."

"Do you think that was appropriate?" Dr. Patterson was sure he would say it wasn't a big deal.

"She must have been uncomfortable, and I felt bad about that."

Dr. Patterson moved on to the hotel situation. "Did you meet with Ms. Whitmore at the hotel she manages asking about meeting rooms?"

Justin snapped back, "I did not. What is this about?"

Dr. Patterson explained to Justin that she was accusing him of pushing her toward a bed in one of the rooms and that she slapped him to get him to stop. Justin was visibly upset.

"This is total crap. I want a meeting with Ms. Whitmore and you to discuss this further."

Knowing that Justin used a Franklin paper planner, Dr. Patterson asked, "Could you please hand me your planner? I want to look at the date in question."

Justin said, "This is my personal planner; no, you may not look at it."

Dr. Patterson had already confirmed with the business manager that the district had purchased the planner for the principal and said, "Justin, the planner is the district's since we paid for it. Hand it here."

Folks who had gone through the Franklin Planning training always put every meeting and phone call in the planner. Justin passed it over to Dr. Patterson, and he went to the date in question—there was a note that he had an appointment with Ms. Whitmore as she had stated.

"Well, Justin. You did have a meeting with Ms. Whitmore. Why did you lie to me?"

"She is a little crazy. First, we looked at meeting rooms, and then she showed me a bedroom. That is all that took place."

Patterson knew it would be her word against his as there were no witnesses. The lying part was a tell for sure.

"Justin, here is what is going to happen: I will place a letter in your file outlining your request for a teacher to pick up your laundry and the situation at the hotel you initially lied about. Ms. Whitmore does not want to make a big deal about this as her daughter is in your student council. The letter will state that if you have another accusation like this one, you will be brought up for termination. The school attorney will draft the letter for your signature."

"This isn't fair, Dr. Patterson!"

"You can attach your version of the situation to the letter in your file and say anything you wish. But you flat out lied to me and didn't want me to see your planner because I would see an appointment you said never existed."

Dr. Patterson got up and excused himself. The letter was given to him the following day. The principal had signed it and did not want to add anything to the letter. From that moment on, their relationship was tenuous. Justin left at the end of the school year for another position.

There was no question that Justin had a problem, and everyone was happy he left. However, Dennis knew he was lying about the hotel situation, and there was probably more to the laundry situation. The teacher was wise not to take the laundry to his home.

Doing the right thing is sometimes challenging but always right. What did you think about this scenario?

PSEL Standards 2, 5, 6, 7, 8

Solution 15

Bananas

Dan's concern at this point was what the school board would say when they heard about this and what the newspaper would write when they caught wind of the prank. He was a proud person and felt terrible that his students would do this to him. However, since it was Friday and there wasn't much they could do until Monday, Dan and the principal decided to let the central office know what had happened in case they received some calls in the meantime.

By Monday, Dan had decided that the speech was not done in a "dirty" manner and that it was one of his students' best. While Calvin exceeded his outlined limits, making a bigger deal out of the matter would only escalate the issue further. The other English department faculty had met with Dan and agreed with his assessment. When Dan met with Principal Swanson again on Monday morning before school, he agreed and let him deal with the class as he saw fit. The central office had not received any calls, nor had the principal.

On graduation day in June, Dan received a gift-wrapped box from his Advanced Speech class, thanking him for being one of the best teachers they ever had. It contained a gift certificate to a local restaurant for him and his wife and a copy of the video of Calvin's speech that really did exist.

PSEL Standards 1, 2, 3, 4, 6, 7

Solution 16

Affair

Sally thought through the situation and went to the central office to visit with the superintendent. She explained her situation and asked if she could contact the school's attorney and run things by him. The superintendent said he had not heard any rumors, but she should call the attorney to be on the safe side. Sally thanked him and went back to her office.

Sally told Peter she wanted him present for the conference call with the attorney. So that afternoon, the conference call was scheduled. The school attorney was excellent and always helped when needed. Sally gave him everything she knew to date.

Ray Sunblad, the attorney, told them, "I would recommend you call Mr. Campbell into the office and ask him why he was parked at the motel with the school vehicle. Push him as hard as you need to until he gives you everything, including whom he was with. He might say it isn't the school's business; if he does, then tell him it became school business when the district's vehicle was parked there. From there, you can issue him a written warning that using a school vehicle for personal use will not be tolerated. I would then bring in the teacher he is rumored to be having a relationship with and give them both a serious verbal warning that the school district may be brought into their personal lives."

Sally thanked Mr. Sunblad and had her secretary take a note to Mr. Campbell and ask him to come to the office during his last-hour planning period. She also had her secretary take a note to Julie Harris, asking her to report to the office after school.

Al Campbell came into the office, and the secretary told him the principal wanted to see him. He went into Sally's office and saw that Mr. Pace was also there. He sat down and said, "Is there something wrong?"

Principal Whitfield didn't mince words. "Please tell me, why did I see the district's station wagon at a motel on Nineteenth Street Saturday afternoon?"

Al squirmed in his chair. "Well, that really isn't any of your business!"

"Oh, but it is since it is a school vehicle. I need to know now, why was it there?"

"I met a friend there who was having some personal problems. That's all." Al was firm.

"We will talk with Julie Harris in thirty minutes in a different office and have you wait here. It will be interesting to hear what she has to say." Principal Whitfield glared at Al.

Al paused and asked how much trouble he was in. The principal told him that if he were honest in his reason for the vehicle being at the motel, he would receive a written warning in his personnel folder for misuse of a school vehicle. That would be all that would happen, except that they would still meet after school and admonish both parties.

Al said that he and Julie were romantically involved and trying to figure out their next steps since they were both married.

Principal Whitfield said, "What you and Julie do on your own time is not any of the school's business unless you bring it into the school, which you did when you used the school vehicle." Shortly after the final bell rang, Julie came into the office. The secretary brought her into the principal's office, where she joined the rest of the group.

"Julie, you are here because the school's station wagon was parked at a motel Saturday afternoon. Al explained that he met you there. What you both do outside of school is none of our business, but the vehicle made this our business. Therefore, I am warning both of you verbally that if your private lives affect your ability to do your jobs, there will be discipline, including possible termination. Are there any questions?"

Neither Al nor Julie had any questions and were dismissed. Principal Whitfield thanked Peter Pace for being present and called the superintendent, telling him a conference summary. He told her he was proud of her and that it would have been easy to look the other way, but that would have been the wrong thing.

This scenario is a perfect example of doing the right thing, which is sometimes difficult but always correct.

PSEL Standards 1, 2, 6, 9

Solution 17

Politics

Superintendent Coring returned to his office and immediately called the school board president and explained what had happened at the elementary school. He asked her to contact the other board members and relay the situation. She was glad no one was hurt and would do so right away.

Superintendent Coring then contacted the school attorney. He explained everything to her, and she said that clearly, a restraining order was a must, and she would work with the police department. She also said she wanted to see the letter sent home to parents before it went out. The principal was told to send a copy of the letter, which she had already started, to the attorney.

The school attorney instructed the principal and superintendent to give the press a copy of the letter being sent home and give them the attorney's name and phone number, as she would be the spokesperson for the district.

As Superintendent Coring expected, before the school day was over, the press had called and wanted to interview the elementary principal and playground supervisor. Superintendent Coring denied the request and had them contact the school attorney.

The court approved a restraining order, and things settled down until a month later when Superintendent Coring received a call from a US senator's office. The aide to the senator explained, "We have received a call from Mr. Charles Gutherie saying that he is no longer allowed to eat lunch at school with his granddaughter or be on school grounds. He is a longtime friend of the senator, and unless he is allowed to visit the school, the senator will contact the state attorney general's office."

Superintendent Coring asked the young aide if she was aware that there was a restraining order on Mr. Gutherie issued by the court. The aide responded, "He did explain that there was one but that it was ridiculous and should never have been issued."

Superintendent Corning firmly stated, "Mr. Gutherie went onto school property during the elementary school recess naked and was arrested. Tell the senator if he still wants to contact our attorney general, I will issue a statement that the senator wants to allow a man who walked naked through an elementary playground with kids present to be allowed back on school property."

The aide said she would call Superintendent Coring back. Ten minutes later, she called and said, "The senator regrets bothering you with this request and will not contact the attorney general's office. Thank you for your time." She hung up.

Everything is a learning experience for administrators. Holden Corning never thought a US senator would get involved with this situation. He was also thankful that the school attorney could deal with all the case inquiries and issues. As he went to bed that night, he thought, "Money well spent!"

PSEL Standards 1, 5, 8

Appendix

Professional Standards for Educational Leaders (PSEL)

Standard 1. Mission, Vision, and Core Values. Effective educational leaders develop, advocate, and enact a shared mission, vision, and core values of high-quality education and academic success and well-being of *each* student.

Standard 2. Ethics and Professional Norms. Effective educational leaders act ethically and according to professional norms to promote *each* student's academic success and well-being.

Standard 3. Equity and Cultural Responsiveness. Effective educational leaders strive for equity of educational opportunity and culturally responsive practices to promote *each* student's academic success and well-being.

Standard 4. Curriculum, Instruction, and Assessment. Effective educational leaders develop and support intellectually rigorous and coherent systems of curriculum, instruction, and assessment to promote *each* student's academic success and well-being.

Standard 5. Community of Care and Support for Students. Effective educational leaders cultivate an inclusive, caring, and supportive school community that promotes the academic success and well-being of *each* student.

Standard 6. Professional Capacity of School Personnel. Effective educational leaders develop the professional capacity and practice of school personnel to promote *each* student's academic success and well-being.

Standard 7. Professional Community for Teachers and Staff. Effective educational leaders foster a professional community of teachers and other professional staff to promote *each* student's academic success and well-being.

Standard 8. Meaningful Engagement of Families and Community. Effective educational leaders engage families and the community in meaningful, reciprocal, and mutually beneficial ways to promote *each* student's academic success and well-being.

Standard 9. Operations and Management. Effective educational leaders manage school operations and resources to promote *each* student's academic success and well-being.

Standard 10. School Improvement. Effective educational leaders act as agents of continuous improvement to promote *each* student's academic success and well-being.

About the Author

Dr. Dewitt Jones grew up in Northbrook, Illinois, a northern suburb of Chicago. He graduated from Glenbrook North High School and then attended Simpson College in Indianola, Iowa, majoring in instrumental music. Dewitt continued his education at Drake University, earning both a master's and a doctorate degree in school administration.